WHAT DO YOU KNOW ABOUT

STEPFAMILIES

PETE SANDERS and STEVE MYERS

Gloucester Press
LONDON • NEW YORK • SYDNEY

Designed and produced by
Aladdin Books Ltd
28 Percy Street
London W1P 9FF

First published in Great Britain in 1995 by Watts Books
96 Leonard Street
London EC2A 4RH

ISBN: 0 7496 1864 7

A catalogue record for this book is available from the British Library.

Printed in Belgium

The publishers wish to acknowledge that the photographs in this book have been posed by models or obtained from photographic agencies.

Design	David West Children's Book Design
Editor	Sarah Levete
Picture research	Brooks Krikler Research
Illustrator	Mike Lacy

Pete Sanders is Senior Lecturer in health education at the University of North London. He was a head teacher for ten years and has written many books on social issues for children.

Steve Myers is a freelance writer who has co-written other titles in this series and worked on several educational projects for children.

CONTENTS

HOW TO USE THIS BOOK

The books in this series are intended to help young people to understand more about issues that may affect their lives. Each book can be read by a child alone, or together with a parent, teacher or helper, so that there is an opportunity to talk through ideas as they come up. The questions that appear on the storyline pages throughout the book are intended to invite further discussion.

At the end of the book there is a section called "What Can We Do?" This section provides practical ideas which will be useful for both young people and adults, as well as a list of names and addresses for further information and support.

INTRODUCTION

TODAY, MILLIONS OF ADULTS AND YOUNG PEOPLE AROUND THE WORLD LIVE AS PART OF A STEPFAMILY.

The number of stepfamilies is likely to keep on increasing. One estimate suggests that by the year 2001 there will be more children living in stepfamilies than in any other kind of family.
This book will help you find out more about stepfamilies: what it means to be part of a stepfamily, the different problems they can face, and how these can be overcome. Each chapter introduces a different aspect of the subject, illustrated by a continuing storyline. The characters in the story have to deal with situations which some of you might experience yourselves. After each episode, we stop and look at the issues raised, and widen out the discussion. By the end you will understand more about stepfamilies, and what can be done to make them work successfully.

BECOMING A STEPFAMILY

THERE ARE MANY DIFFERENT TYPES OF FAMILY. STEPFAMILIES ARE JUST ONE PARTICULAR KIND.

A stepfamily is formed when two adults decide to live together, and one or both of them has children from a previous relationship. It may be that the adults are separated or divorced from their ex-partner, or that a husband or wife has died. Some stepparents are married, some live together and there are some same sex stepparents. Stepfamilies are just like any other family but because they are created from an already established family or families, they face specific challenges of their own.

It can take a long time to adjust to being with a new group of people, especially if this includes new stepbrothers or stepsisters. Some stepfamilies are very large, particularly if both adult partners have children. Some children become part of two stepfamilies, if both of their natural parents form new relationships, although they will probably live with just one family on a regular basis.

It can be difficult coping with the changes involved in becoming part of a stepfamily.

▽ Jane and her friends, Anita and Vicky, were chatting in the playground.

△ Simon told Jane that his dad and her mum were going to get married.

▽ Jane was miserable all day. After school she rushed home and confronted her mum, Jo, who told her Simon was telling the truth.

△ Jane's parents, Jo and David, had been divorced for two years.

◁ Jane felt really angry. She stormed out of the room. Jo heard the front door slam.

Why do you think Jo found it difficult to tell Jane?

Jane is upset about the way she has found out about Jo's marriage to Andrew.
Jo realises that she should have prepared Jane for this news. Even when children have become used to their parent's new partner, the idea of the relationship becoming permanent may still be a shock. Changing the structure of the family is a big step. It is important that everyone is honest about what is happening, and has the chance to talk about their feelings.

Jane has responded to the news by losing her temper.
When people feel angry or upset, their emotions can sometimes get the better of them. Their feelings may be so strong that they block out everything else. Reacting immediately to a situation, as Jane has done, does not solve anything or make the problem go away. It will make things easier if you give yourself time to think calmly about the situation, and to talk about it with the other people concerned.

Many young people, like Jane, find it hard when one of their parents forms a new relationship.
It can seem as though the absent parent is being betrayed. This is equally true when one parent has died. If your parents have divorced or separated they may lead completely independent lives. Some will remain friends but others may not want to see or talk to each other. This doesn't mean that they will love their children any less. Whatever their feelings for each other, they will always be your parents. Most divorced or separated couples continue to love their children a great deal.

STEPPARENTS

GETTING TO KNOW AND ACCEPT NEW PEOPLE, AND GROWING TO LIKE THEM, TAKES TIME.

Just as we cannot choose our natural parents, we usually have little say in the choice of stepparent.

Many children like their stepparents right away. Sometimes, however, the relationship is more difficult. Young people often compare their new stepparent with their natural one. Because the newcomer is "stepping in" to take on the role of a parent whom the children may still love and miss, children often feel resentful towards the new parent. They may see this person as trying to replace the absent parent and as a threat to their love or memory of them. The children may think that they shouldn't talk about their natural mother or father. These feelings can be particularly true if their natural parents' relationship ended as a result of one of them meeting this new person. Many stepchildren come to love and care about their stepparents a great deal but this does not mean that they have to love their natural parents any less.

It can also be difficult for stepparents, particularly if they haven't had children of their own. Just as you are getting used to your new parent, he or she is also getting used to you! Everybody involved needs to give each other time.

Sometimes children may blame their stepparent for the absence of their natural mum or dad.

▷ An hour later, Jane hadn't returned. Worried, Jo called Anita's house and spoke to her mother, Sandra.
I WAS GOING TO CALL YOU. YES, SHE'S HERE. SHE'S PRETTY UPSET I'M AFRAID.
I KNOW. I'M GLAD SHE'S SAFE. WE'LL COME RIGHT OVER.
▽ Andrew thought it best for him to collect Jane on his own.
SHE'S ANGRY AT YOU, AND THE TWO OF US HAVE ALWAYS BEEN FRIENDS UP TO NOW.
MAYBE YOU'RE RIGHT. I SHOULD HAVE TALKED TO HER THIS MORNING. SHE MUST BE FEELING REALLY HURT.
I KNOW THEY'RE DIVORCED, BUT I STILL BELIEVED ONE DAY MUM AND DAD WOULD GET BACK TOGETHER AGAIN.
◁ Up in Anita's room, Jane had told her what had happened, and how she was feeling.
I KNOW HOW HARD IT IS. I WAS REALLY UPSET WHEN MUM MET NEIL.
▷ Jane was surprised. She had thought Neil was Anita's dad.
NO, NEIL'S MY STEPDAD. THIS IS MY REAL DAD. I DON'T SEE HIM VERY OFTEN.
WHY? WHAT HAPPENED TO HIM?
▷ Anita told Jane how her parents used to argue all the time. Eventually they divorced. Her father met someone else and now lived abroad.
I MISS HIM SOMETIMES. IT TOOK ME AGES TO LIKE NEIL. BUT I CAN TELL THAT MUM'S MUCH HAPPIER WITH HIM.
WELL NOBODY'S GOING TO REPLACE MY DAD. I DON'T KNOW WHAT MY MUM SEES IN ANDREW.

▷ Jane turned around and found Andrew standing in the doorway.

▽ Andrew had bought her a personal stereo.

▷ Later that evening, Jo told Andrew he should not have given Jane the present.

Do you think Jo is right?

Jane is comparing Andrew to her father.
It can be tempting to idolise people and to remember past events as better than they actually were. However, this only makes it harder to accept and welcome someone else into the family. Rather than judging your new parent against your feelings for your natural parent, it is more constructive to base your feelings for somebody on the way he or she behaves towards you. Each person is different from everybody else.

Anita found it hard to get used to Neil as her new dad.
This is understandable, as she knows she already has a dad. It can be difficult to know what to call your new parent. Some young people are happy to use "mum" and "dad". Others prefer using first names. It is important that you and your stepparent talk together about what you will both feel happiest calling each other.

Jo criticised Andrew for having bought a present for Jane.
Sometimes adults do buy presents to try to win the affection and loyalty of children. Parents who no longer live with their children may try to make up for their absence by doing this. New parents are often anxious to gain the loyalty and friendship of their step-children in a short space of time. They may think that treats and gifts are a quick and easy way to do this. Although this may seem to do no harm, in the long term, buying affection is not an effective way of building up a positive relationship. It takes time and effort to develop lasting friendships and relationships.

STEPBROTHERS AND SISTERS

BEING A BROTHER OR SISTER IS NOT ALWAYS EASY, EVEN IN ESTABLISHED FAMILIES.

Getting used to each other can be especially difficult for new stepbrothers and stepsisters.
The arrival of a stepbrother or sister may make you feel that your role in the family is being threatened. Stepbrothers and sisters may try to manipulate situations to their own advantage. If it seems that one has more privileges than another, this can lead to arguments and accusations that things are unfair. Stepchildren may compete for the attention and affection of different parents. Age differences can also cause problems. For instance, you might suddenly find yourself having to look after a much younger brother. Or you may see an older stepsister being allowed to do things which you are not. This can lead to feelings of resentment and jealousy.

Given time, most stepbrothers and sisters find a way to get along with each other.

▷ The following weekend, Jo and Andrew had planned to take the whole family away together.

◁ Simon and his older sister, Pam, noticed Jane was moody.

▽ When they arrived at their hotel, Simon, Pam and Jane learned they would be sharing a room.

▷ Later that morning, they all went to the beach.
WHY DON'T WE ALL PLAY A GAME?
THAT'S A GREAT IDEA. COME ON, PAM.
THERE'S AN ODD NUMBER FOR A GAME. COUNT ME OUT.
DO YOU THINK SHE SHOULD GO OFF ON HER OWN?
SHE'LL BE ALL RIGHT. SHE'LL BE BACK IN TIME FOR LUNCH. COME ON THE REST OF YOU, LET'S PLAY.
▽ Pam refused to join in, and decided to go for a walk.
YOU PLAY SILLY GAMES IF YOU WANT TO, SIMON. I'M OFF.
HERE, SIMON. CATCH.
NOT YET. I'M NOT READY.
GOOD POINT, SIMON.
I TRIPPED, OR I WOULD HAVE GOT THAT.
◁ Simon felt unsure about what to do. But he decided to play with the others.
WELL DONE, SIMON. I DIDN'T KNOW YOU COULD PLAY SO WELL.
THERE'S NO NEED TO GO OVERBOARD MUM.
▷ Jane had not enjoyed the day. Even though she was sharing a room, she felt very lonely.
I WISH THINGS WERE LIKE BEFORE. I'LL NEVER GET USED TO THIS.
Do you think Jane is right?

Because she is an only child, Jane is finding it very hard to adapt to the new situation.

If you are not used to having to take into account the feelings of brothers and sisters you might think that you have lost your special status in the eyes of your mum or dad. Whereas before you had their undivided attention, now others will make demands on their time and affection. If you are worried about this, it can help to talk about your fears with your natural parent.

Jane is feeling jealous, because Jo was being affectionate towards Simon.

Jealousy is a destructive and painful emotion which, in the end, only hurts everyone concerned. It can help to talk openly about your feelings to your parents. Remember that there is no reason why the arrival of someone new into the family should change the way your parents feel about you.

To most people, having their own space and privacy is very important.

Simon, Pam and Jane are not happy with having to share the hotel room. They are each used to having their own rooms. It can feel very threatening if you think that you are going to lose your own space. Sometimes, however, in order to find the best solution for everyone, compromises have to be made. Even when people have to share the same space, they can still respect each other's privacy. It is important that everybody is allowed time to be alone if they want to.

MIXED LOYALTIES

IF TWO ADULTS REALISE THAT THEY NO LONGER HAVE STRONG LOVING FEELINGS FOR EACH OTHER, THEY MAY DECIDE TO SEPARATE OR DIVORCE.

Their children, however, may be left with powerful feelings towards both parents.

This is perfectly understandable. Living with just one of your parents does not mean that you will feel any less loyal or loving to the other. If one or both of your parents forms a new relationship, you may feel that you are betraying your natural parent if you like the newcomer. This is not the case. Sometimes young people like their stepparent more than their absent natural parent. Although this can feel very confusing, there is nothing wrong with liking someone. You may find, however, that no matter how hard you try, you do not like your stepmother or stepfather. You may feel that you cannot be honest about this, because to do so would be disloyal and would hurt your natural parent. All of these conflicting emotions can be equally as true if one of your parents has died – you may still feel very close to them and feel that you are betraying their memory. It often helps to talk to someone you trust about your emotions.

Stepchildren and stepparents can become good friends.

▽ Once a month, Jane spent a weekend with her dad, David.
BYE, JANE. SEE YOU ON SUNDAY.
SO THAT WAS ANDREW. HE LOOKS A BIT WEIRD TO ME. WHAT'S HE LIKE?
HE'S OKAY, I SUPPOSE.
△ David asked lots of questions about Andrew and his family.
ANYWAY, HOW WAS THE WEEKEND ON THE COAST? I BET IT WASN'T AS GOOD AS WHEN WE ALL USED TO GO AWAY TOGETHER. REMEMBER THE FUN WE USED TO HAVE?
I DON'T THINK YOU'RE VERY HAPPY WITH THE NEW ARRANGEMENT. I THINK YOUR MOTHER'S BEING SELFISH. SHE SHOULD HAVE THOUGHT MORE ABOUT HOW YOU WERE GOING TO FEEL.
▷ On the way to school, Jane told Anita about the weekend.
I DON'T REMEMBER ALL THE TIMES DAD TALKED ABOUT. BUT THEY'VE GOT TO BE BETTER THAN NOW.
I WISH I COULD LIVE WITH MY REAL DAD.
MAYBE YOU CAN. WHY DON'T YOU TALK TO HIM ABOUT IT?
◁ Jane decided to phone her dad.

Jane sees her father, David, once a month.
When a child's parents separate or divorce, an arrangement is often made for the child to have access to both parents. This can be very difficult for stepfamilies. Just as the new family is trying to get settled, every so often the young people will leave to spend time with their natural mum or dad. This break in routine can cause tension and can itself take time to get used to.

Jane is confused by what David has said.
In some cases, parents will try to turn their children against their ex-partners, by talking about them in a negative way. This can make the young people concerned feel confused and unsure of themselves. It can make them feel as if they should only have loving feelings for one of their natural parents. This should not be the case. Manipulating people's feelings in this way is sometimes known as "emotional blackmail". Both children and adults are capable of this. In the long term, however, this behaviour succeeds only in causing bitterness.

Jane feels like a go-between for David.
This can happen when two adults separate, and no longer communicate with each other. Although they are living apart, they may still be interested in what is going on in the other person's life, particularly if he or she has begun a new relationship. It can put a lot of pressure on the young people if one parent is asking them to give out private information.

FEELING EXCLUDED

WE ALL NEED TO HAVE A SENSE OF BELONGING, AND WANT TO FEEL IMPORTANT TO THE PEOPLE WE ARE CLOSE TO.

Adults who are forming a new relationship sometimes forget this. Relationships take time to develop. New partners are sometimes so involved with each other that they do not seem to pay much attention to anybody or anything else. It can be very difficult to accept that there are other important people in your parent's life. At first, you may feel left out and rejected, but just because your mum or dad has an important new relationship, it doesn't mean that you are any less special to them. You may feel resentful and lonely if you are used to spending a lot of time with your parent and it suddenly seems as if they have no time for you. Some young people react by becoming moody or withdrawn. Children might behave quite badly to get their parent's attention. However, it is often only the newness of the adult relationship which is the cause of the apparent change. After a while, once they have got to know each other better, the focus of their attention may alter. Your natural parent will want to include you in the new relationship and will want you to get to know and like their new partner.

Feeling left out can be a very lonely and painful emotion.

▽ Jo and Andrew were making plans for their wedding.

▽ In the living room, Simon found Jane in tears.

▽ Jane told Simon she was feeling lonely.

▽ Later, Jane decided to go round to see Anita.

▽ Anita told Jane that her mum was going to have a baby.

△ The wedding was only a month away.

Do you think Anita is right to be worried?

Anita has some doubts about the idea of a new baby.
At first, many young people think of a new baby as a threat to their status in the eyes of their parents. For stepchildren, it can be particularly worrying. They know that the baby will be the natural child of their parent and stepparent. They may fear that as the child of different parents they will be second best to the new baby.

Jane is upset, because she feels let down by her natural dad.
Situations don't always work out the way we would like, and people sometimes do things we don't want them to. It helps to remember that we cannot always control everything and everybody in our lives. Seeing the situation from the other person's point of view can make it easier to deal with the feeling of being let down.

Both Jane and Simon are finding the changes in their lives difficult and painful.
Simon is missing his mum, and feels rejected by Andrew. Jane is no longer sure where she fits in the family. When you are not in control of the relationships around you, you may be unsure about your feelings for other people, and theirs for you. This can make you feel isolated and lonely. It is important to realise that the other people involved may be feeling exactly the same way.

ACCEPTING CHANGE

YOU ONLY HAVE TO THINK ABOUT WHAT YOU COULD DO AS A BABY AND WHAT YOU CAN DO NOW, TO UNDERSTAND THAT CHANGE IS A NATURAL PART OF ALL OUR LIVES.

We are able to choose some changes for ourselves. Others happen outside our control.

Some people find adapting to change easier than others. Very young children have fewer problems than older ones, because they do not have all the experiences and memories to look back on. Becoming part of a new family is an enormous change. It can take a long time to adjust to. People know that things will never be the same. They are often frightened that this means that their lives will not be as happy or fulfilling as they were before. For this reason, they may resist the change, and try to hold on to the past. It just takes time and effort on everybody's part to make change a successful and rewarding experience.

Stepchildren might have to move house. They may worry that they will lose touch with their friends and everything which is familiar to them, but this need not happen.

▽ Six weeks after the wedding, Andrew had come down with 'flu.
I'M GLAD YOU WEREN'T IN THIS STATE ON THE WEDDING DAY.
SO AM I. THANKS, JANE. I DON'T KNOW WHAT I'D DO WITHOUT YOU. PUT THE TRAY DOWN HERE.
MUM WILL BE UP IN A MINUTE. PAM'S GOING OUT AGAIN, AND THEY'RE HAVING ONE OF THEIR LITTLE CHATS.
▽ Pam and Jo were arguing about what time Pam had to be home.
YOU'RE NOT MY MOTHER. DAD WOULDN'T BE AS STRICT. HE'D LET ME STAY OUT LATER.
I DON'T CARE. I WANT YOU HOME BY 10·30. NO ARGUMENT.
▽ Later that evening, Anita came round.
THIS IS A SCAN OF THE BABY. I EVEN LISTENED TO ITS HEARTBEAT AT THE HOSPITAL. I HOPE IT'S A GIRL.
AND WHAT'S WRONG WITH BOYS?
SHALL WE TELL HIM?
YOU CERTAINLY SEEM HAPPIER NOW.
WELL, IT'S STILL A BIT STRANGE, BUT I'M GETTING USED TO IT. ACTUALLY, IT'S QUITE NICE HAVING SIMON TO TALK TO.

Pam and Jo are still finding it difficult to get along.
Adults often have different ideas about discipline. Some are very strict, others may be more easy-going. Many children find it hard to come to terms with their parents' authority over them, particularly as they get older. You may think that you should be able to decide for yourself. Having stepparents tell you what to do may seem particularly unfair. You may feel that because they are not your natural parent, you do not have to listen to them. Remember that most parents impose rules because they care about you.

It can be difficult to accept changes that we do not choose for ourselves.
At first, Jane was worried about what becoming part of a stepfamily would mean, but has now begun to realise that there can be good things in change – for example, new opportunities and friendships.

Anita is excited about the new baby.
The feelings you have when first faced with change are often different from those you have when you have had a chance to think about the situation. This is why reacting in the heat of the moment is not always the best way to deal with something.

ATTITUDES TO STEPFAMILIES

AS WELL AS DEALING WITH PROBLEMS WITHIN THE FAMILY, STEPFAMILIES CAN FACE ADDED PRESSURE FROM OUTSIDERS.

Relatives and friends often have their own very different ideas about what makes a family, and how families should behave. They may try to impose their views on others. For instance, some people believe that divorce is wrong, and that remarriage should not be allowed. They might cause problems for a couple in a new relationship, where one or both of them is divorced. On the other hand, if two adults choose to live together without marrying, they may face criticism from those who disapprove of this arrangement. Some religions have very strict rules about divorce and remarriage. When adults from different races or backgrounds form intimate relationships, there might be opposition from people who believe that this should not happen. This kind of pressure is not helpful for a new family. Only those within the stepfamily can decide what is right for them.

Each culture and religion has its own attitude to divorce and remarriage.

▷ The end of term play at school was based on the story of Cinderella.

▽ The following week, Andrew and Jo came to see the play.

▽ The next day, Vicky made fun of Andrew's appearance.

Stories like Cinderella often show stepparents as being evil or wicked.
Fairy tales such as this are usually very old. They are based on the idea of a "stranger" disrupting a happy family. Although this image is still popular in fiction, it has no basis in reality. Most members of a stepfamily take time and care to get to know each other – perhaps more than other families.

Vicky is using the stereotypical view of a stepfamily to make fun of Jane.
A stereotype is a very general image applied to a group of people, regardless of the individuals involved. Vicky's remarks have nothing to do with what Jane's family is really like. Making comments about people without thinking them through can be very hurtful. It is important to challenge and question negative attitudes and mistaken ideas in the way that Simon has.

The relationships between members of a stepfamily can be just as loving and caring as those of any other kind of family.
Jane realises this, and has stuck up for Andrew. Most parents and stepparents are deeply concerned about their children's well-being. They are committed to providing the best for them. There need not be any conflict between the way you feel about your stepparent and the way you feel about your natural parents.

SUCCESSFUL STEPFAMILIES

STEPFAMILIES THAT WORK WELL HAVE DEVELOPED A SENSE OF TRUST AND CO-OPERATION.

To do this successfully, there is a need to understand and respect not only your own feelings, but also those of others.
Communicating effectively with other family members is very important. It can be easy to forget that it is okay to disagree occasionally. Everybody makes mistakes, and we all have faults. Learning to forgive and not to hold grudges is a way to make sure that barriers are not created between different members of the family. It helps to remember that everyone involved is getting used to the new situation. Some stepfamilies find it helpful to agree ground rules. Others who are having problems may find that counselling can help them. However, being part of a stepfamily can be very rewarding. Members of a stepfamily find that the process of accepting change and the experience of learning how to establish new relationships can also be useful in other areas of their lives.

You may find that you become really good friends with the other members of your stepfamily.

▽ Jane had just returned from seeing her dad, David.
YOU'RE BACK EARLY. I SUPPOSE YOUR DAD WAS IN ONE OF HIS MOODS AGAIN?
NO HE WASN'T. WE HAD A GOOD TIME. HE LOVED THE VIDEO OF THE SCHOOL PLAY, AND WANTS TO SHOW IT TO HIS FRIENDS.
I WISH YOU WOULDN'T TALK ABOUT DAD LIKE THAT.
SORRY. I'M GLAD YOU'RE GETTING ALONG.
▽ Pam was meeting a friend in town that evening.
CAN'T WE MAKE IT 11.30 TONIGHT?
NO, BUT SINCE IT'S A WEEKEND, WE'LL COMPROMISE AND MAKE IT 11.00.
11.00 IT IS. SOUNDS FAIR TO ME.
SO, DID YOU TWO HAVE A GOOD DAY?
YOU BET. YOU SHOULD COME WITH US NEXT TIME.
▷ Suddenly, Andrew had an idea.
I'LL TELL YOU WHAT WE SHOULD DO. WE SHOULD BOOK ANOTHER WEEKEND ON THE COAST.
GOOD IDEA. I'VE A FEELING WE MIGHT ALL ENJOY IT A BIT BETTER THIS TIME.

As Pam and Jo have realised, compromise is sometimes necessary. Arguing and refusing to give in at all does not solve anything. It is more constructive to listen to each other's point of view and to try to understand how the other person feels. Finding a way of living together that suits everyone can turn out to be very simple.

Jane is upset about Jo's attitude towards her dad. Adults often find it difficult to realise that children have the right to make up their own minds about people. Those who are divorced or separated sometimes assume that their children share their views about their ex-partner. Although an adult may be starting a new relationship, the bond between young people and their absent parents can remain just as strong.

Each member of a stepfamily has a responsibility to make the relationships work. This takes time and effort on everyone's part, as Jane and Simon's family has discovered. If everybody is prepared to make an effort and contribute, being part of a stepfamily can be great fun.

WHAT CAN WE DO?

HAVING READ THIS BOOK, YOU WILL UNDERSTAND MORE ABOUT THE NATURE OF STEPFAMILIES, AND ABOUT THE PROBLEMS THEY CAN FACE.

You will know that being part of a stepfamily is perfectly normal, and can be just as fulfilling as being part of any kind of family.
It is important not to rush things. All relationships take time to develop. If you are getting to know a new stepmother or stepfather, try not to compare them to your natural parents. Everybody is different from everyone else. It helps if you can accept your new stepparent for him or herself. We all have different needs and wants, and may not always agree how to behave in certain situations. It is important to try to be honest about your feelings.

National Stepfamily Association
72 Willesden Lane
London NW6 7TA
Tel: 071 372 0844 (office)
071 372 0846
(counselling services)

Relate
Marriage Guidance
Herbert Gray College
Little Church Street
Rugby CV21 3AP
Tel: 0788 573241
Relate has local offices throughout Britain.

ADULTS CAN HELP TOO, BY UNDERSTANDING THE PRESSURE THAT CAN BE PUT ON YOUNG PEOPLE IN A STEPFAMILY.

Children can have very mixed emotions about being a member of a stepfamily.

It may be tempting to try too hard. Stepparents need to give stepsons and daughters time and space to get used to the new situation. Adults and children who have read this book together may find it helpful to share their views and ideas. Anyone who would like to find out more about stepfamilies, or who is experiencing problems they would like help with, should be able to obtain information, advice and support from the organisations listed below.

Carers' National Association
20-25 Glasshouse Yard
London EC1A 4JS
Tel: 071 490 8818

Childline
Freepost 1111
London N1 0BR
Tel: 0800 1111

Youth Advisory Service
Brook Centre
233 Tottenham Court Road
London W1
Tel: 071 323 1522

National Family Mediation
9 Tavistock Place
London WC1H 9SN
Tel: 071 383 5993

The Parent Network
44-46 Caversham Road
London NW5 2DS
Tel: 071 485 8535

National Council for the Divorced and Separated
13 High Street
Little Shelford
Cambridge CB2 5ES
Tel: 0533 700595

Family Welfare Association
501-5 Kingsland Road
London E8 4AU
Tel: 071 254 6251

Children's Protection Society, Australia
Tel: 010 613 450 3566

Family Resource and Network Support
Beresford Avenue
Croydon Park
Sydney
Australia
Tel: 010 612 799 4333

INDEX

Photocredits
All the pictures in this book are by Roger Vlitos apart from pages: cover: Anne Layle; 4 Pete Bennett; 24 Frank Spooner Pictures.